GOD IS ON YOUR SIDE

DR. LINDA WASHINGTON

ISBN 978-0-578-77329-2 (paperback)

ISBN: 978-0-578-77330-8 (ebook)

DEDICATION

To GOD ALMIGHTY, who brought me out of the pit of hell into His marvelous light.

To my beloved paternal grandparents, Rev. Joseph Washington and Ida Washington, both whom I never met, but often thought about.

To my beloved maternal grandparents, Henry Douglas Moody and Matilda Moody, who died before my birth.

To Mama Sista, my step-grandmother, who came to visit me in rehab and prayed over me in the Holy Ghost. I truly believe the Kingdom of GOD heard her prayer and is why I'm still alive today.

To my parents, Shedrick Dennis Washington and Carrie Bell Moody Washington Jackson, as well as my stepfather, Elmo Jackson.

To "Aunt Susie" Parker, an educator, teacher, and mother, who was dearly loved.

To "Uncle Herman" Moody, a Las Vegas retired police officer who was a hero and great community leader.

To my beloved brothers and sisters, Charles, Sybil, Pomey, Ethel, Shedrick Jr., and Lucinda.

CONTENTS

INTRODUCTION

In this book, you will find many topics, mostly dealing with my experiences surrounding addiction, rejection, and low self-esteem. It has taken me several years to open up about certain incidents that occurred, but I'm glad that GOD gave me the strength to write about them. So much weight has been lifted off my shoulders.

Who am I? Only a sinner saved by grace through obedience to the Son (Jesus). I hope that my transparency will prevent others from going down a dangerous path in life that can lead to hardship, sickness, family losses, limited finances, abandoned dreams, and stifled creativity. Mostly, I want people to be saved from eternal damnation.

Many times, I use the names GOD and Jesus to strongly emphasize that calling on the sovereign GOD is the answer. The focus is to direct specific attention to GOD and GOD alone. I don't want you to focus on me, but I invite you to glean from my personal experience, knowing that you are not alone or forgotten. You are loved, fearfully and wonderfully made. If GOD delivered me and others, you are not exempt from the mercy, grace, lovingkindness, and forgiveness that grants you another chance in life.

Most of all, giving up is not the answer. Receiving validation from others can be a hindrance. Failing at something is just an opportunity to get back up and try again. GOD wants us to persevere through trials and tribulations, no matter how painful they might be. My prayer is that whomever this book reaches, their eyes of understanding will be enlightened, and their hearts will be open to receive the words that GOD speaks to them through this book. It's ok to be transparent as long as it will help someone to become better.

CHAPTER 1
NAKED TREE

One day in February, still feeling nature's winter effects, I was sitting in my upstairs bedroom looking through the window blinds. The not-so-bright sunshine was overshadowed by the cloudy sky. I found myself glaring at a tall, newly trimmed raspberry tree through the windowpane.

Suddenly, I realized the branches had no leaves or any fruit due to the season we were in. There was an awaiting harvest that had not yet come. That image seemed to capture my attention. I realized that the Spirit of GOD Almighty was speaking to me regarding that barren tree.

During our lives, we go through times where everything is for a "season." That type of tree only blossomed during the spring and summer seasons. Although it was a beautiful tree, it could create a messy yard once the berries started falling to the ground. Catch the words I used: beautiful and messy, similar to the human image.

The Bible tells us about Jesus healing a blind man who could partially see before he was totally healed. Jesus asked the blind man, "What do you see?" The blind man replied, "I see people looking like trees." The image of a tree is symbolic. A tree is no good unless it produces after its own kind, whether it be fruit or just leaves. As humans, we are required by GOD to produce the goodness of His love, kindness, gentleness, and godliness before others. When we produce love, others can see the image of Jesus in our lives.

While we are fearfully and beautifully made, human lives can become very messy.

Seven events that can cause a messy life:

1. Choosing the wrong path
2. Unhealthy relationships
3. Unhealthy thoughts
4. Unforgiveness
5. Substance abuse
6. A contentious spirit
7. Unbelief

Do you struggle with any of the above? If so, write a prayer asking GOD for help with your expectations. Pray that

GOD will bless the intellect of the mind, body, soul, and spirit. Ask GOD to touch your reasoning, judgment, and motives, which will keep you from making detrimental decisions.

Everything is for a "season" in life. Sometimes we have to wait on GOD for our blossom to appear. Just like the raspberry tree, it can only blossom in its designated season.

What does it mean to wait? Does it mean to sit still and do exactly nothing? No, not at all. Let's define the word *wait* (transitive verb): to stay in place, in expectation of or (intransitive verb): to remain stationary in readiness or expectation.

To wait is an act of preparation with expectations concerning what you are believing GOD for. While waiting with expectations, there must be a desire to wait on GOD in a serving capacity. For example, GOD instructs "serve the Lord GOD with all your heart, mind, and soul." There should be a strong desire for GOD by asking Him, "How can I serve you today?"

To wait on GOD Almighty, we must be willing servants by showing love toward others, helping someone in need, having godly morals, and demonstrating integrity in the likeness of our Creator. Staying focused on GOD produces healthy thoughts, provides encouragement and promotes good work through servanthood.

Seasons like spring, summer, autumn, and winter are marked by weather patterns and daylight hours, resulting from the earth's changing position regarding the sun. In our walk, while we are waiting and depending on GOD, we go through spiritual seasons. We have ups and downs and trials and tribulations, which are a part of life.

There are going to be seasons of harvest during which we can experience the overflow of GOD's blessings. Sometimes there may be a wilderness season where GOD will bring us to a place that only He can aid us through. We are tested the most when in the wilderness. It is where our spiritual development, strength, faith, patience, courage, and a deeper love for GOD emerges.

The Bible says in Psalm 23 that "The Lord is my Shepherd, He makes me lie down in green pasture; He leads me beside still waters; also, He restores my Soul unto His righteousness." Whatever season you are in, just hold on to GOD the Father, GOD the Son, and GOD the Holy Ghost.

JOURNAL

Explain your wilderness/desert experiences? Describe
how you cope with waiting on GOD.

_____

_____

_____

_____

_____

_____

_____

_____

_____

_____

_____

_____

_____

_____

_____

_____

_____

_____

_____

_____

_____

_____

_____

PRAYER

Almighty,

I thank you for allowing me to look up to you, who can do exceedingly and abundantly. I put my total trust in you with every season of my life. Thank you for giving me the strength and courage to be steadfast in my wilderness season. Without you, Lord Jesus, nothing is possible, but with you, everything is possible in your name.

Amen

CHAPTER 2
ONCE UPON A TIME!

A certain person had a deep, longtime, intimate love affair in a very common way. This affair had become the main source of all life problems. In the beginning, the love affair made everything appear wonderful. It always made itself available by supplying whatever this certain person needed. This love affair held on and would not let go. It was soothing to the soul, but the love affair could no longer remain hidden. It had to expose its evil intent - deception

The love affair waited patiently to get this person exactly where it wanted them to be. Suddenly, it attacked the brain, the mind, the body, and the soul. It spoke with uncertainty, isolation, self-destruction, loneliness, hopelessness, and no desire to pursue love and happiness. This love affair moved rapidly and went for the kill. But, through the Grace of GOD, a cry of desperation went out into the spirit realm. GOD heard and saved that person from the captivity of their soul. This "love affair" was named **Addiction**.

At 20 years old, I was introduced to alcohol. It led me to wrestle with an addiction for about 18 years. Who was to blame? I wanted to claim that I was a victim of circumstance, also known as generational curses passed from one generation to another. Could it be that I was destined for this through DNA?

In my younger days, I remember hearing others in the family say that my mother occasionally drank while carrying me. If so, I am almost positive it was not done intentionally. As a matter of fact, in those days, people were not educated on the risk or danger of alcoholism, especially to an unborn child.

Generational curses follow a pattern starting with immediate parents, then their parents, and so forth. If only my fore parents had insight about alcoholism and how it affects the intellect and reasoning of the brain, vitality of the organs, functioning of the nervous system, and most importantly, the entire soul.

The Bible says, "My people are destroyed for lack of knowledge." Not knowing the dangers of substance abuse can have a lifetime effect on individuals and their families. The signs include living in delusion (a pretentious world), seeking unhealthy attention or validation, desiring love from strangers, and having false courage.

I could not function unless I was intoxicated. I had a daily ritual after work that included excessive drinking and listening to the same old song over and over again. I was hurting mentally and experienced paranoia, depression, and social problems. Thankfully, I survived what I put myself through.

Each morning I would awaken with a terrible hangover (dizziness, vomiting, and headache). I never could understand how I managed to make it to work on time. My social behavior suffered at work, with my family, and in my relationships. I had unprofessional behavior (speaking out of turn, showing a lack of interest, poor work ethic, etc.) I could not get along with anyone. I played the blame game. *They are talking about me. Why am I not accepted? Why are they looking at me?* My focus was off. One moment, I was upbeat, and the next, I was down. I would not discuss my business with anyone.

Addiction can really take control of the mind, judgment, and reasoning. During that time, I was in my last stage of alcoholism. My consumption of alcohol was high. I started drooling from the mouth, and my tongue curled up to the point that I had to take my fingers and press on my tongue for relief. I didn't even realize that I was showing symptoms of a stroke. I had two DUIs during my addiction period, but I thank GOD that there were no injuries or deaths involved.

With my second DUI in October 2000, I was at work feeling depressed from not being invited to an event with company employees. I did something very unusual that evening. I stopped at a local bar. I was a closet drinker who drank at home, so bars were not appealing to me.

After having several drinks, I proceeded to get into my car. I had a difficult time backing out of the parking lot because I was so intoxicated. Everything seemed like a fog. I headed toward a two-lane, dark highway. I managed to get two blocks up the street before I noticed red lights flashing behind me. Even though I was arrested, GOD protected my life and protected others.

I reached the point of a turnaround in my life. GOD Almighty intervened as I was placed in a medical recovery program facility for the third time. By that time, I had hit rock bottom.

Miraculously, during my fourth week of recovery, I heard Jesus speaking with a soft, gentle, loving, and powerful voice. He said, "You are healed." Until then, I had never heard the voice of GOD in my life. I replied, "Really, Lord?" GOD said, "I have removed the craving of alcohol from your body, removed the desire of alcohol from your eyes, and removed the taste of alcohol from your tongue."

I was so joyful hearing this from Jesus! I asked, "How can I pay you back?"

GOD replied, "Serve Me." At that moment, I accepted Christ Jesus into my heart.

I was in a medical recovery program at that time and could not share this with the counselor. The Lord wanted me to continue with the program because I would learn how the addiction affected every organ in the body and the brain. Jesus gave me another chance at life, and He will do the same for you!

Food for Thought

Substance abuse will destroy your dreams, goals in life, and eventually will take your life. Receiving help through counseling and therapy counselors helped me realize that I had developed a relationship with my drug of choice: alcohol. Yes, a relationship.

It may sound strange, but this "thing" was a seducing spirit that took complete control of me. One moment it gave me a Dr. Feel Good vibe, and the next, it had me twirling as though I was in some sort of tornado. I had been in several dysfunctional relationships, but the invisible enemy I had unknowingly entertained was the worst decision I had ever made.

Through counseling, I was able to see that I was living a life of delusion with false hope, false courage, and a false sense of self-sufficiency. The devil had me fooled, blindsided, and set up for eternal destruction. If I could have turned back the clock on my actions, I would have done so in a heartbeat.

No matter how bad your situation may be, GOD can defeat every obstacle in your life. Just cry out to GOD. Do you know that GOD hears the cry of a soul that is in trouble? Remember that GOD is with you at all times. There is nothing too hard for GOD.

The Bible says, "Behold, I am the LORD, the GOD of all flesh: is there anything too hard for me?" (Jeremiah 32:27) Therefore, it's time to take an inventory of self and learn the difference between a healthy and unhealthy relationship.

The meaning of **addiction** is: (noun) the state of being enslaved to a habit or practice or to something that is psychologically or physically habit-forming, as narcotics, to such an extent that its cessation causes severe trauma. Latin addictiōn-(addictiō) a giving over, surrender.

Types of addictions range from everyday drugs like alcohol and cocaine to behaviors like gambling and stealing. Some types of addiction are specified in the Diagnostic and Statistical Manual of Mental Disorders (DSM-IV-TR), while others are more controversial and have been identified by some addiction professionals[1].

While there are many types of addictions, I will narrow it down to two categories:

1. **Mental**: The addiction is in the brain. The addict has thoughts and memories of using the substance.
Thought patterns and obsessions hold the addict in the grips of their addiction.
2. **Physical:** The body is dependent on the substance and will crave it along with unhealthy relationships.

JOURNAL

What thoughts are you struggling with? Do you
struggle with letting go of certain thoughts that come
into your mind? Do you know that you can bind the
devil and every evil thought through the Word
of GOD?

What the Bible Says About a Troubled Mind

"Casting down imaginations, and every high thing that exalteth itself against the knowledge of GOD and bringing into captivity every thought to the obedience of Christ." - 2 Corinthians 10:5

"Many are the plans in the mind of a man, but it is the purpose of the Lord that will stand." - Proverbs 19:21

"A merry heart doeth good [like] a medicine: but a broken spirit drieth the bones." - Proverbs 17:22

"I will restore you to health and heal your wounds 'declares the Lord." - Jeremiah 30:17

"Jesus graciously welcomed them and talked to them about the kingdom of GOD. Those who needed healing, he healed." - Luke 9:10-11

"Lord, you know how I long for my health once more. You hear my every sigh." - Psalm 38:9

"Yes, I will bless the Lord and not forget the glorious things he does for me. He forgives all my sins. He heals me." - Psalm 103:2-3

JOURNAL

Do you listen to your body? What is your body telling you today?

_____

_____

_____

_____

_____

_____

_____

_____

_____

_____

_____

_____

_____

_____

_____

_____

_____

_____

_____

The Creator formed humans and breathed His Divine breath of life, during which man became a living soul. This is known as the intellect of the soul (mind, body, and spirit). Humans were not given life to treat themselves as trash, garbage, or behave like animals. We are to praise, worship, and glorify GOD, knowing that GOD does not make junk. We are to treat our bodies like the temple of GOD.

What the Bible Says About the Physical Body

"I beseech you therefore, brethren, by the mercies of GOD, that ye present your bodies a living sacrifice, holy, acceptable unto GOD, which is your reasonable service." - Romans 12:1

"What? know ye not that your body is the temple of the Holy Ghost [which is] in you, which ye have of GOD, and ye are not your own." - 1 Corinthians 6:19

"I will praise thee; for I am fearfully and wonderfully made: marvelous are thy works; and that my soul knows right well." - Psalms 139:14

Ways to Show Self-love in a Godly Manner

1. Keep GOD the Father, the Son, and the Holy Ghost as the head of your life.

2. Love others.
3. Be good to yourself.
4. Confess all wrongdoings unto GOD.
5. Be thankful for the highs and lows in your life.
6. Pray without ceasing.
7. Overcome negative beliefs about yourself.
8. Avoid perfectionism.
9. Discard your negative filter.
10. Never call yourself names.
11. Do not assume the worst can happen; know that Jesus is your Rock.
12. BIND fear.

JOURNAL

What ways can you demonstrate gratefulness unto the Creator?

_____

_____

_____

_____

_____

_____

_____

_____

_____

_____

_____

_____

_____

_____

_____

_____

_____

_____

_____

_____

_____

_____

Prayer

Dear GOD,

You are so awesome! Thank you for your all-powerful love (agape). You knew me before the creation of the earth and before I was fashioned in my mother's womb. I come to you humbly to show me how to care for my mind and body. Bless me with your divine wisdom concerning how to give my body as a living sacrifice, holy and acceptable unto you. Most of all, I repent from not honoring the life and body you have blessed me with. From this day on, I will give You the highest praise as I eagerly learn to love me.

Amen

---

1. www.samhsa.gov

CHAPTER 3
PURPOSE OF ALLEGIANCE

"O' Thou my GOD, how I honor you. I glorify you with the highest praise. Thank you, Jesus, for allowing me one more chance at life. You brought me up from the grave and pulled me out of a world of darkness when I was on my way to a burning hell. You heard my cry, and because of your grace and mercy, you came to my rescue and delivered my soul. How can I repay a GOD so Powerful?"

Jesus answered, "Serve Me."

What is Allegiance?

Allegiance means to give a promise to be loyal or the action of being loyal to someone or on someone's side. For instance, swearing that you will follow the laws and commandments of the Trinity.

GOD first commanded, "Thou shalt love the Lord thy GOD with all thy heart, and with all thy soul, and with all thy strength, and with all thy mind; and thy neighbor as thyself." (Luke 10:27)

Secondly, we should seek Him daily through prayer, fasting, and His Word. The Word of GOD says, "Ye are my friends, if ye do whatsoever I command you." (John 15:14) Meaning, surrender all unto the Almighty.

Personal Experience

After making several attempts to be substance-free from my alcohol and drug abuse over the years in a recovery program, nothing seemed to work for me. I discovered that my lack of success was tied to the fact that I had not hit rock bottom. Once I had incurred my second DUI, GOD had truly caught my attention. He spared my life and the lives of others.

For 18 years, I suffered from a hangover almost every morning. I knew I was officially an addict. The signs and warnings were there. My friend would always tell me, "You need to stop drinking. It's altering your personality. That's why you can't hold a job! You're always having confrontations with others." I thought I was in a safe zone because I was only drinking at home. The enemy will trick and deceive you when you are in the **H.A.L.T.** phase of your life.

Hungry: I was hungry for a change in my life. I did not realize how spiritually bankrupt I had become. Once full, I was now totally empty of all GOD's goodness.

Angry: I became angry when I thought about what others had done to me. I remembered all of the negative words that had been spoken into my life as a child. I was upset that I had put all of my energy into unhealthy relationships and consistently looked for love in the wrong places.

I was angry because I was dealing with verbal and physical abuse in every aspect of my life. I was angry because I realized that all of my hopes and dreams had been demolished. I was angry because there was no way out for me.

Lonely: I chose to be alone. It was a safe place for me. In my mind, I figured that no one would be able to hurt me again if I never let anyone get close.

Tired: I was tired of self-abuse. I had tried to do it my way for years and found myself continually failing. I was dealing with loss in more ways than one. I had to juggle the death of my parents and close friends and the failure of a relationship. I was tired of living! I mean, really. What was the use?

During my addiction, I'd always looked for validation from others, especially in the workplace and my family circle, which had caused me to live in a false world I created for myself. I medicated myself to hide my true feelings. I did not want anyone to see how damaged I became. Because of my behavior issues, everyone viewed me as being difficult to get along with. However, there is something I need to share. Hopefully, it will help you.

One day, my co-workers were getting together for a social gathering after work. Everybody was invited except for me. This troubled me greatly because I had an acceptance issue. Deep down, I wanted to be a part, but my communication and social skills were nonexistent due to a lack of self-confidence and substance abuse.

Upon leaving work, I felt a strong sense of rejection and decided to stop at a local bar instead of going straight home. This course of action was very unusual for me. I was a closet drinker who chose to drink all my troubles away at home.

After consuming three drinks, I immediately rushed myself to the restroom. I began to experience symptoms that made me believe I was having a stroke. My tongue felt as though it was having muscle spasms. My mouth started to twitch on one side of my face. I was extremely frightened and too intoxicated to call out for help. Once I got myself together, I walked out of the restroom, still intoxicated, and preceded out the door to my car, knowing full well that I was in no condition to drive.

As soon as I drove out of the parking lot and turned the corner, I saw red flashing lights behind me. I pulled over and asked GOD to intervene. I had no idea that in spite of my poor choices, GOD would still show grace and mercy towards me. GOD used the police officers to arrest me, which saved my life and so many potential others. I am certain that if GOD had not intervened by allowing my arrest, I would not be alive today.

Do not allow destructive substances and corrupt individuals to have power over you. Learn how to love GOD and yourselves. Let GOD validate you. Let GOD accept you. Let GOD approve you. The Bible says, "What shall we then say to these things? If GOD be for us, who can be against us?" (Romans 8:31) Do not worry about what others think of you.

Lastly, always remember to pray! Prayer is the answer! Pray daily without ceasing! Pray about everything! Pray for GOD's divine protection and healing over your life. Ask Him to bless you with sound reasoning and judgment when making decisions.

Prayer

Father GOD,

*For whoever is reading this prayer, I ask that they totally submit to you. Deliver them from the validation, acceptance, and approval of others. Keep them from feeling unloved. Help them make the best decisions. Remove self-hatred and self-doubt from their souls. Your Word says, "that you have not given us the spirit of fear; that you have given us **power** to Trust in GOD, **love** that cast away all fears and a **sound** mind to lean toward your understanding in all situations." We trust and believe all confirmation comes from you.*

Amen

JOURNAL

Do you have an acceptance issue? If so, why?

_____

_____

_____

_____

_____

_____

_____

_____

_____

_____

_____

_____

_____

_____

_____

_____

_____

_____

_____

_____

_____

_____

_____

CHAPTER 4
A CRY FROM THE OTHER SIDE OF MIDNIGHT!

"Prepare you the way of the LORD; make straight in the desert a highway for our GOD." (Isaiah 40:3) Isaiah brings a word of comfort to Jerusalem and foretells the coming of our Lord and Savior. This word applies to all believers today.

Psalm 56:8 says, "You have collected all my tears in Your bottle. You have recorded each one in your book." The Bible tells us GOD collects our tears in a bottle. He knows what you're going through. He looks up to Jesus and casts all your burdens by prayer, faith, and trust. Do not doubt GOD. He hears the cry of the people because the cry of desperation, hurt, loss, and pain comes from the one place he understands better than anyone else – the heart. GOD thinks deeply about His people and weeps for them.

*Therefore, when Jesus saw her weeping, and the Jews
who came with her weeping, He groaned in the spirit
and was troubled. And He said, "Where have you laid
him?" They said to Him, "Lord, come and see." Jesus
wept. Then the Jews said, "See how He loved him!" -
John 11:34-36*

GOD honors obedience, a thankful heart, and those who
offer themselves as a living sacrifice unto Him. That's why we
must examine our hearts daily. It's important to be honest with
ourselves and acknowledge all of our weaknesses.

Sin sometimes places us in a state of desperation, causing
us to make poor decisions in life. Making wrong choices has
severe consequences that will bring you down to your knees.
GOD hears the cries of the lowly and performs His divine
intervention in the valley, but only once they have repented
and turned toward His marvelous light.

It's time for the people to make a pathway for GOD. It's
time for us all to confess that Jesus is Lord and believe with
our whole hearts that He is the one who died on the Cross and
resurrected to ensure we could live eternally. GOD desires for
us all to return to him. He has consistently granted us grace
and mercy. He has given us another chance. Now is the time
where we should open our hearts and follow His will.

Remember, you became a living soul once GOD breathed into
you. Everything you are and everything you have comes from

GOD. It is only right that we accept Jesus Christ as our Savior before we leave Earth. Why wouldn't you want to spend eternity with the very one who chose to create you and send His only Son to die for you? It is now time for you to make that decision.

We are living in a time where people are sleepwalking in a dark and dying world. It's time to wake up because midnight is soon to come. GOD does not desire to see you perish nor destroy you; you are GOD's creation, beautifully designed with His signature. YES, you!

GOD has never forgotten you. He has never thrown you away. These are your own thoughts that you created because of the positions your sin may have put you in. We can be our own worst enemies at times by the people and the situations we chose to entertain.

The Bible says the world consists of the following three (3) entities that are **not** of the Father:

1. The lust of the flesh
2. The lust of the eyes
3. The pride of life

I recall my mother telling me from one bad relationship to another, "You are not thrown away. There is someone for you." One day GOD revealed to me that "someone" was Him. He told me that he would be able to love me in a way that no human ever could. Throughout my life, I've discovered that this is called agape love.

Agape love extends beyond human love. It is a love that will not stop loving. It is a love that will not abuse you or walk away from you. It is a love that will not attack you or curse you. A love that will never lead you on or leave you lonely. It will not attack your character or curse your existence. It will not do anything but supply you with goodness, compassion, gentleness, lovingkindness, and an abundance of life. Jesus is a keeper!

"The LORD is your keeper; The LORD is your shade at your right hand." - Psalms 121:5

JOURNAL

What does it mean when a cry is heard? Can you hear
when the Lord is speaking? Why is it important to hear
from GOD?

_____

_____

_____

_____

_____

_____

_____

_____

_____

_____

_____

_____

_____

_____

_____

_____

_____

_____

_____

_____

_____

_____

_____

Various Meanings of the Word, Cry

1. To utter inarticulate sounds, especially of lamentation, grief, or suffering, usually with tears.
2. To weep; to shed tears, with or without sound.
3. To call loudly; shout; yell (sometimes followed by out).
4. To demand resolution or strongly indicate a disposition.
5. To give forth vocal sounds or characteristic calls, as animals; yelp; bark.
6. (of a hound or pack) to bay continuously and excitedly in following a scent.
7. (of tin) to make a noise, when bent, like the crumpling of paper.
8. (used with object) cried, crying.
9. To utter or pronounce loudly; call out.
10. To announce publicly as for sale; advertise.
11. To cry one's wares.
12. To beg or plead for; implore.
13. To cry mercy.
14. To bring (oneself) to a specified state by weeping.

Midnight

The Biblical translation of the word *midnight* is the darkest hour before day; in the middle of the night; an_intense darkness or gloom. Midnight is symbolic of a dark and dying world that never brings about permanent solutions because of the Fall of Adam at the beginning of creation. This is evidence that one bad decision can have a lifetime effect that will carry on from generation to generation.

The Wilderness of Life's Trials and Tribulations

"For a great door and effectual is opened unto me, and there are many adversaries." - 1 Corinthians 16:9

All preparation occurs in the desert. Desert Training, GOD! Sometimes, GOD will allow circumstances to occur just so that He can get your full attention. When this happens, GOD is equipping you for a brighter future.

Do you remember the time where you felt an urgency to cry out? To be heard? Do you remember when you searched aimlessly for answers to questions that plagued your thoughts? You may have wondered if anyone cared or if anyone was even there.

Sometimes desert training can seem very lonely and spiritually painful. However, GOD's Word states, "There hath no temptation taken you but such as is common to man: but GOD is faithful, who will not suffer you to be tempted above that ye are able; but will with the temptation also make a way to escape, that ye may be able to bear it." (1 Corinthians 10:13)

Trust GOD in the desert process. There is a plan and

purpose that He is grooming you for. I guarantee you will not be the same when you come out. You will be much stronger and wiser with a strong hunger for Him. Always remember that GOD will not allow you to suffer more than you can bear. Trusting GOD is the key factor.

You were created to allow GOD to be the center and the head of your life in everything you do. Whatever your desires, whatever your goals, seek Christ for his divine wisdom. Remember, you are loved by a GOD who cries for you. You are HIS CREATION!

JOURNAL

What are some obstacles in your Desert Experience?
Rejection? Sickness? Mental anguish? Homelessness?
Write about your "desert experience" here.

_____

_____

_____

_____

_____

_____

_____

_____

_____

_____

_____

_____

_____

_____

_____

_____

_____

_____

_____

_____

_____

_____

Prayer

Lord,

Thank you for giving me a voice to cry out to you, a cry that only you can hear and understand. A cry that came from a land of isolation, which is called the desert. A cry that was different from any other cry of desperation. Lord GOD, you are the Creator, the beginning and the end, the Alpha and Omega. What an omnipotent, omniscient, and omnipresent God you are.

Amen

CHAPTER 5
THE PAST IS GONE

Stop running in the name of Jesus! Become steadfast, unmovable. Take a stand and face your past.

> *"Therefore, my beloved brethren, be ye steadfast, unmovable, always abounding in the work of the Lord, forasmuch as ye know that your labor is not in vain in the Lord." - 1 Corinthians 15:58*

What does it mean to be steadfast? What does it mean to be unmovable? How can you abound in the works for GOD? How can someone know that their labor in Christ Jesus isn't in vain?

I recall an old school song I used to listen to as a teenager by the Supremes called *Stop in the Name of Love*. In the Greek, *eros* means romantic love. Well, GOD gave me an epiphany from this song. He said, "Stop running from my love! Let go and let GOD. STOP trying to live without my love. I came so that you may have LIFE on earth. ALL THINGS ARE POSSIBLE WITH GOD."

Lean On God

Can you hear GOD telling you to "STOP" in the name of HIS love? The agape love? The highest love? GOD will not lead you on. GOD will not break your heart. GOD is forever, everlasting, infinite.

Stop leaning on self-ability and start leaning on the power of Jesus. Without the power of the indwelling of the Holy Spirit in us, we are nothing. However, when we have the Spirit of Life within, we become new creatures. GOD has desires and promises for us, but He asks that we be strong through difficult times, knowing that our trials and tribulations will come to pass.

The enemy wants to keep us in the past with doubts and negativity. However, in Christ, we are free from doubts. The power of GOD Almighty will stand tall within us if we just stop and come to terms that our past has been washed away.

The only place we should run is into His arms. Run from the ways of the world and choose to run this spiritual race instead. Let go of all the bitterness, resentment, character defects, and seek GOD daily for HIS guidance, deliverance, protection, and wisdom.

Spiritual Observation

"If any man be in Christ, he is a new creature: old things are passed away; behold, all things are become new." - 2 Corinthians 5:17

In this passage, GOD is confirming unto the people of GOD at Corinth through Apostle Paul that He will make you whole and wash away all your wrongdoings and bring you into a new life.

"The prayer of faith shall save the sick, and they shall raise him up; and if he has committed sins, they shall have forgiven him." - James 5:13

Another confirmation of the promises of GOD is that by faith, all things are possible with Jesus. You are forgiven and have been adopted into the family of Christ.

"The Spirit you received does not make you slaves, so that you live in fear again; rather, the Spirit you received brought about your adoption to sonship. And by him we cry, "Abba, Father." - Romans 8:15

The promise here is that upon accepting our Lord Christ Jesus in our lives, we are no longer in the bondage of the worldly systems, which bring about mental torment. Christ came to set you free and to give you a new name with everlasting life into HIS KINGDOM.

What are your desires? What are your dreams? What has GOD instilled within you as your gift? Do you feel driven to serve GOD on the inside of you, no matter how hard you try to resist it? It's time to receive GOD's promises. STOP and take a STAND against all oppositions in prayer and supplication, according to Philippians 4:19, which states, "But my GOD shall supply all your need according to his riches in glory by Christ Jesus."

Forgiveness will squash the burdens of hurts from others and release you from years of mistakes. Stop letting the past haunt you, keeping you stuck and feeling unforgiven. Remember, we serve a forgiving GOD. There is nothing too big for GOD. Let Jesus take you through the healing process.

The battle comes from the hurt of pain and loss, which can leave a lasting effect on the intellect of the soul. You may even have asked, "Why me? How can I overcome this and go on in life?"

Well, I have your answer. You can overcome and progress through life with Jesus. Remember, the battle was already won at the Cross, where the blood of Jesus was shed.

"All things are possible in Christ Jesus, who can strengthen me." - Philippians 4:13

Look at that mountain of hurt, pain, and trauma and start

speaking to it. *I'm an overcomer.* Speak life into your situation. Do a faith walk by believing GOD will move your mountains of disadvantages out of the way.

> *"For verily I say unto you, if ye have faith as a grain of mustard seed, ye shall say unto this mountain, remove hence to yonder place, and it shall remove, and nothing shall be impossible unto you." - Matthew 17:20*

Trust in the Lord and lean not on your own understanding. Watch for the movement of GOD. Remember, you aren't exempt from trials and tribulations, but through GOD, the battle is already won.

PRAYER

Heavenly Father,

In the name of your Son Jesus, I give all thanksgiving unto you for this day and being the Source of my life. With adoration, you are GOD all by yourself. I thank you, Lord, for seeing me when you came to earth to endure the CROSS. Thank you, Lord, for protecting me when I was running from you. Because of your mercy and lovingkindness, I am alive today. Please hear my cry. Heal and deliver me from myself and the past. This day, my Lord, I choose to let go, to be still, and wait on you. All of my trust is in you.

Amen

CHAPTER 6
NEVER TOO LATE TO FORGIVE

Picked Out to be Picked On

As a young woman with so many dreams, I always daydreamed about being married, having children, and working as a career woman with great success. However, in my aging adulthood, I realized none of my dreams came true. *What happened? What did I do wrong in life? There must be something wrong with me.*

Well, sometimes, we can unconsciously hold on to something that affects the decisions we make in life. Holding on to a hurtful situation can interfere with your dreams, self-confidence, and perseverance. You can walk through life in a state of depression without even realizing it. Life should not be this way.

I remember being called ugly and chased home when I

was in middle school during the 1960s. During this era, there was a lot of drinking and chaos in black families. Many of these families had financial issues, which made it difficult for them to survive. Most kids during those times only expressed themselves by hurting one another. It was just the thing to do.

One day I came home from school crying because some kids had beat me and tore my blouse off of me. I did not like to fight, but my mother had told me that the next time I better fight back, or she was going to deal with me. I was very skinny then with a pair of bow legs. I also wore glasses, which didn't help. I was always being called "four eyes" or having them knocked off of my face. Unfortunately, I wasn't taught to embrace who I was. My parents were more concerned about ensuring that all of the bills were paid.

As I progressed into junior high school, there was a young boy who I knew in passing named Joe C. He was the boy that most of the girls dreamed about being in a relationship with. I wasn't most girls.

Someone with my same initials had written "LW + JC" on the walls of the girls' bathroom. This meant that these two individuals were dating. Since I was a loner, I had never been interested in him or anyone else for that matter. However, one particular day as I walked to class, Joe C. walked toward me with a group of his female admirers, convinced that I had written that we were dating on the wall in the bathroom. He approached me and asked why I lied on him. He told me to stop using his name without permission in front of everyone.

I tried to tell him that I had no idea what he was referencing, but he refused to listen to me. He cut me off by saying, "You are not my type. I would never be with your bowlegs and ugly self." He added a few bad names to go along with it.

This was devastating for me as a thirteen-year-old girl. His words affected my mental state for years. It was such a trying time for me. It was hard being laughed at every day that I went to school. I was so embarrassed.

I am not exactly sure how I made it through that situation. There was no one I could talk to. I learned how to bury it in my subconscious mind. However, suppressing the incident only made me a very angry individual.

Several years later, I had gotten in touch with old friends whom I knew in junior high school and discovered that Joe C. had died from an overdose. It made me wonder if he was under the influence of narcotics at the time he said those harsh words to me. There was a big epidemic of taking pills amongst the black communities during those times.

As I continued to walk and serve Christ Jesus, I realized that I must forgive those in my past who caused harm. During my recovery process, I learned one profound way that anyone can use to forgive someone they may never see again. By writing an imaginary letter of forgiveness with a seal and no return address, you are spiritually forgiving and releasing your hurt.

The Bible says, "Therefore, since we are surrounded by such a great cloud of witnesses, let us throw off everything that hinders and the sin that so easily entangles. And let us run with perseverance the race marked out for us" (Hebrews 12:1)

Letter of Forgiveness

Joe C,

> *Over the years, I often thought about that incident and what a bad effect it had on me. I carried it on my shoulders for so many years that a spirit of vexation hovered over me. It left me feeling very insecure. I was a seeker of validation full of anger, and I did not love myself.*
>
> *Now that I am older, much wiser, and living for GOD, I can make sense of it all. Being very young, we can make bad decisions without realizing how it may hurt someone else. The image of you stating those harsh words is still visible in my mind, but now I realize you did not know any better. You were young, popular with the girls, and just being a teenager.*
>
> *Today, I choose to release you and the bad memory by letter through the spiritual realm. I forgive you and pray that you are resting in peace.*

In this life, there will be people who pick on you. Do not let the actions and opinions of others have power over your destiny. Keep your eyes and heart on the one who has all power while you run this race.

JOURNAL

Do you have a letter of forgiveness to write? Write it here and begin your healing.

_____

_____

_____

_____

_____

_____

_____

_____

_____

_____

_____

_____

_____

_____

_____

_____

_____

_____

_____

_____

_____

_____

_____

_____

_____

PRAYER

Dear GOD,

Thank you for bringing me into your knowledge, understanding, and wisdom. I now know the importance of forgiving others. I realize that we all have weaknesses and are sometimes blind to the hurt we can inflict on others. Today, I choose to forgive people, situations, and the past, in Jesus' name.

Amen

CHAPTER 7
THE DANGER OF H. A. L. T

HALT is a principle used in recovery. It is a method to control impulses and urges. The following are synonyms for the word *halt*:

cease, stop, finish, discontinue, terminate, conclude, come to an end, come to a halt, come to a stop, end, come to a standstill, be over, be abandoned, pause, be broken off, be suspended

Hungry

Are you in need of a change in life? Have you ever felt empty inside? Are you searching for something to fulfill the most inner part of you? Have you come to realize that you are spiritually bankrupt?Spiritual hunger can put you into a very long season of dryness depending on the types of choices you make. The void can be so unbearable that you look for love in all the wrong places for all the wrong reasons. You will find yourself seeking satisfaction from tangible things that cannot love you in return.

Have you ever felt numb or lost interest in doing the things you used to do? Do you know that you are alive, but find yourself struggling to enjoy life and the ones around you? Suddenly, you realize that nothing on earth can satisfy the urgency of despair, void, and lack of spiritual nourishment other than GOD. What is causing the void in your life?

Angry

Where is this emotion coming from? You show the world that you are happy, bubbly, and outgoing. However, you are living a life of denial. You wake up every morning and place a mask over your face to hide your true feelings.

I did not want to face the hurt, pain, and trauma I had endured from others or the negative words that had been spoken into my life as a child. I put all my energy into unhealthy relationships just to find someone to love me. I dealt with verbal and physical abuse in every aspect of my life. My dreams, hope, and life were almost demolished due to the poor choices I made.

Lonely

It was a safe place for me. I figured no one would ever hurt me again if I did not let anyone get close to me. My drug of choice had become my best friend. The enemy tricked me into believing that alcohol was the one thing that would not hurt me. The Word of GOD states, *"My people are destroyed for lack of knowledge" (Hosea 4:6).*

Tired

After years of self-abuse, trying to do it my way, I knew that there had to be a change. For years, I dealt with loss. I experienced the death of my parents and some of my closest friends. I was forced to end a relationship with someone who really didn't love me. I got to the point where I just wanted to give up on life.

Giving up is not an option. As your life continues, always keep a clear conscience. H.A.L.T. is a dangerous place where you become a sitting duck for the devil to steal, kill, and destroy by taking away your blessings, your dreams, and your life.

Take the time to admit why you are having these negative emotions. You need to examine yourself before GOD, being honest about your weaknesses and faults.

Strengthening Process

When we are in spiritual recovery, we already feel deprived due to the process of healing. It does not come overnight. When in the healing process, make sure that you are partaking in Jesus' goodness and lovingkindness. If you are in spiritual recovery, this isn't a time for unnecessary deprivation. If we starve physically, emotionally, and spiritually, we will find that we will become weary and unable to adequately fight our battles.

The Power of Confession

Self-examine and confess your faults to yourself, to God, and to someone you trust.

"If we confess our sins, he is faithful and just to forgive us our sins, and to cleanse us from all unrighteousness." - 1 John 1:9

Confess your wrongdoings to the Lord after self-examination.

"Confess your faults one to another, and pray one for another, that ye may be healed. The effectual fervent prayer of a righteous man availeth much." - James 5:16

Jesus uses confession to set us free from spiritual bondage and hidden sins that seem to linger and keep us in shamefulness. Jesus wants us to come clean so that He can cleanse us inside out. I must admit that confessing wrongdoings to another person can be difficult, but if we let GOD, He will put a specific person (spiritual, counselor, or sponsor) on our path who can identify with what we have experienced.

Let your trust be in God. Be obedient to the commandments of the law and keep a prayer life. Take ownership of your wrongdoings by admitting the to the ALMIGHTY GOD.

JOURNAL

What deprives you of enjoying your life?

_____

_____

_____

_____

_____

_____

_____

_____

_____

_____

_____

_____

_____

_____

_____

_____

_____

_____

_____

_____

_____

_____

_____

_____

_____

_____

JOURNAL

How do you define the word *confession*? Why is it important?

_____

_____

_____

_____

_____

_____

_____

_____

_____

_____

_____

_____

_____

_____

_____

_____

_____

_____

_____

_____

_____

_____

PRAYER

Father GOD,

The GOD of Abraham, Isaac, and Jacob, the Most High infinite Creator, you loved the world so much that you made it possible for each of us to be redeemed by the Blood. GOD, I just want to thank you for salvation, forgiveness, and healing. Thank you for healing me from the adversary of addiction and the pain I imposed on others. Lord GOD, you are the reason why I am still here today. I do not deserve all of your goodness and lovingkindness. Thank you, Lord GOD, for supplying all of my needs unconditionally unto me. Humbly, I will continue to give all the praise, all the glory, and all the honor unto the ALMIGHTY GOD.

Amen

CHAPTER 8
YOU ARE INVITED

Lord GOD, I surrender all. GOD ALMIGHTY! You saved my life.

After deep studying in the Word of GOD, I fell into a deeper relationship with GOD. He had given me another chance at love, and I loved Him for doing so. When GOD delivered me from my addiction, I was able to identify with the lame man at the gate.

Peter and John approached a man who had been lame since birth, not realizing GOD was getting ready to perform a miracle in his life. Peter said in Acts 3:6-8, "Silver and gold have I none; but such as I have, I give you: In the name of Jesus Christ of Nazareth rise up and walk." They took the lame man by the hand, and he stood up, feeling strength in his feet and ankles. Then he stood and entered with them into the temple, walking, leaping, and praising GOD.

Well, that's exactly what I did during my fourth week in recovery, for that was the first time in my life that I heard the voice of GOD speaking to me. From that very moment, I finally knew what true LOVE was. Just like the lame man in the spirit, I saw myself jumping, leaping, and praising GOD.

Just as GOD told the lame man not to tell anyone what had occurred, He spoke the same words to me. I was in recovery in a medical facility where religion was not used as part of the treatment. They would not understand because it was so divine and spiritual. I know that it is said that once you are an addict, you are always an addict. However, I am here to tell you that I am delivered. GOD delivered me and revealed that my spiritual gift was to be an evangelist.

During my spiritual process, GOD was quickly taking me deep into His Word. Unbeknownst to me, my notes were actually sermons. My official spiritual training started with me attending Sunday School, Bible Study, and prayer services. As time progressed, the Lord GOD ALMIGHTY led me to the mission field, which consisted of me witnessing to the homeless and those with mental illness. Because of the indwelling of the Holy Spirit, the Lord trained me to teach and showed me evidence of His divine power as he transformed lives before my eyes for an entire decade.

One day after teaching bible study to the Women's Ministry, I passed by the Mission Chapel and felt an unction to inquire about it. The door to the Chapel opened to me, and I delivered my first message to the homeless. I was so nervous, but as time went on, it became easier and easier.

GOD allowed me to see that His people desperately needed spiritual food. The natural food nourishes the body, but the spirit needed to be fed. The Spirit of GOD said, "Preach Luke 14: 16-24 with the theme, 'Eating at the King's Table.'" As I stood before the people of GOD with praise and thanksgiving, allowing the Holy Spirit to minister to them, I proceeded to explain that our GOD is a Savior, Deliverer, Healer, Protector, and King of all Kings. I let them know that they are loved and invited them to join Him and have everlasting life.

The book of Luke tells us how people rejected GOD and came up with excuses for why they could not come to the invitation. So, GOD told His faithful servant to go and bring in the Gentiles. Those were the lost, cripple, blind, maned, hopeless, broken, unloved, and mentally sick. They were all invited to the banquet. We are the modern-day Gentiles. We are invited! Hallelujah!

Come to the Water

Nicodemus inquisitively asked Jesus one night, "How can I come out of my mother's womb twice?" Think about it on an individual level. When you accepted Christ into your life, your state of being was in darkness until your heart was receptive to receive Christ in your life. We must come to Jesus with the same inquisitive spirit and ask, "Jesus, how can I be made over as a new creature? How is this possible?"

We must come to Christ with an open heart just as Nicodemus did. So, this is what Jesus said unto Nicodemus, "Verily, verily, I say unto you, 'Except a man be born of water and of the Spirit, he cannot enter the Kingdom of GOD.'" It's amazing how Jesus uses the natural things of life to explain the spiritual realm. Jesus goes on to explain those who are born of the flesh are physical, and those are who are born of the spirit are spiritual. After your physical birth, you must go through your spiritual birth.

JOURNAL

How would you describe a spiritual birth?

_____

_____

_____

_____

_____

_____

_____

_____

_____

_____

_____

_____

_____

_____

_____

_____

_____

_____

_____

_____

_____

_____

_____

Come to the Bread of Life

All of our spiritual nourishment comes from the Word of GOD, which comes by atonement. We must cleanse ourselves and separate ourselves from worldly desires. When Jesus was in His forty days of fasting, Satan thought he could seduce Jesus into temptation, but Jesus said, "Man shall not live by bread alone, but by every WORD that comes from GOD ALMIGHTY."

Jesus was setting an example for us to live by. Every attack from the enemy on our daily walk should be combated with the Word of God. It is the spiritual bread that will keep us whole, unmovable, and steady on this spiritual journey. The Bible also says, "I am the Bread of Life, who that comes to me shall never hunger and who that believe on me shall never thirst." (John 6:35.) What a powerful and loving GOD! You would be foolish not to accept this invitation.

JOURNAL

Are you hungry for Christ? What are some spiritual
desires that you have?

_____

_____

_____

_____

_____

_____

_____

_____

_____

_____

_____

_____

_____

_____

_____

_____

_____

_____

_____

_____

_____

_____

_____

When we think of meat, many of us think of a well-cooked steak. According to the United States Department of Agriculture (USDA), there are three main cuts of beef.

- **Prime** – a cut produced from the young, well-fed cattle.
- **Choice** – a cut from the loin and the rib.
- **Select** – a cut that is known to be leaner.

Naturally, feeding the physical body is a temporary fulfillment. After so many hours, the center part of the brain called the *hypothalamus*, which is located under the midline of the brain, sends a "hunger signal" to the body.

However, there is another interpretation of **U. S. D. A.** that is purely spiritual.

- **U** stands for *unite* and *understand*.

"Teach me thy way, O Lord: I will walk in thy truth: unite my heart to fear thy name." - Psalm 86:11

What is in your life that you need GOD to help you with? How will you commune with GOD to touch your heart?

- **S** stands for *statute*. GOD's Law (statutes) is found in Exodus 20.

"With Elohim, there are boundaries. GOD will allow us to go so far with HIM, it's foolish for humans to kick against the Stone of Salvation." - Psalms 91:12

The statute of GOD ALMIGHTY should be with us from sunrise to sunset, each and every day unto eternity and forevermore.

- **D** stands for *dedicate*.

"I beseech you therefore, brethren, by the mercies of God, that ye present your bodies a living sacrifice, holy, acceptable unto God, which is your reasonable service. And be not conformed to this world: but be ye transformed by the renewing of your mind, that ye may prove what is that good, and acceptable, and perfect, will of God" - Romans 12:1-2

We belong to and came from GOD, and on this journey, we must consecrate ourselves by fasting, and praying for others, acknowledging our failures, and seeking His forgiveness, deliverance, and guidance.

- **A** stands for *atonement*.

"Yet he was merciful; he forgave their iniquities and did not destroy them. Time after time he restrained his anger and did not stir up his full wrath." - Psalms 78:38

Only the GOD ALMIGHTY has the power to restore sinful humans to their rightful place with GOD through acceptance of believing in Christ Jesus, who was sent to pay a debt for us on the Cross.

JOURNAL

Write some of God's statutes that you are familiar with.

_____

_____

_____

_____

_____

_____

_____

_____

_____

_____

_____

_____

_____

_____

_____

_____

_____

_____

_____

_____

_____

_____

_____

_____

_____

_____

JOURNAL

What are some ways that you can dedicate yourself
to God?

_____

_____

_____

_____

_____

_____

_____

_____

_____

_____

_____

_____

_____

_____

_____

_____

_____

_____

_____

_____

_____

_____

_____

JOURNAL

Write a prayer of Thanksgiving below.

_____

_____

_____

_____

_____

_____

_____

_____

_____

_____

_____

_____

_____

_____

_____

_____

_____

_____

_____

_____

_____

_____

_____

_____

_____

CHAPTER 9
180-DEGREE TURNAROUND

To be spiritually fed, we must take a different approach by meditating on the Word of GOD.

*"He that **eat my flesh** and **drink my blood**, dwell in me, and I in him. (57) As the living father have sent me, and I live by the Father: so he that **eat me**, even he shall live by me." - John 6:56-58*

Jesus was a "divine human," meaning He came to earth in the form of man but was sent by GOD the Father to save a condemned world. The flesh represents goodness, and the blood represents truth and holiness. Also, flesh and blood signified the bread and wine at "The Last Supper."

Jesus is reminding us that His flesh is the Bread from

Heaven, which is The Word of GOD. The Bible is the spiritual nourishment that feeds our souls.

We must accept that Christ is "the Truth, the Way, and the Light, no man comes to the Father, but, by me" (John 14:6). All of our needs will be supplied by the WORD of GOD if we believe. This includes healing, comfort, and victory that is free from emptiness.

Our daily prayers should consist of **ACTS**:

- **A**dmiration: Adore Elohim GOD Almighty.
- **C**onfession: Confess our wrongs; seek forgiveness from GOD.
- **T**hanksgiving: Be thankful unto GOD for everything – the good, bad, highs and lows; keep a thankful heart.
- **S**upplication: GOD will supply your needs according to His will if you believe and trust Him.

Why would Jesus say, "drink my blood?" In a physical sense, it would appear to be insane and gross. Let's compare the difference between *natural* blood and *spiritual* blood.

Natural blood is essential to the human body. This blood circulates through our body and provides essential substances like oxygen and nutrients to the body's cells. However, there is no substitute for human blood. It cannot be made or manufactured. The only replacement is from another human, which is known as a blood donor.

Natural blood has four components:

1. Red blood cells consist of 40% - 45% of our blood volume, which is generated from our bone marrow at a rate of four to five billion per hour. They have a lifecycle of about 120 days in the body.
2. Platelets control bleedings whenever a wound occurs. The blood vessel will send out a signal, and the platelets will receive that signal and travel to the affected area.
3. Plasma is the liquid portion of your blood. It is yellowish in color and made up mostly of water. It also contains proteins, sugars, and hormones. It delivers water and nutrients to your body tissues.
4. White blood cells, known as leukocytes, account for 1% of your blood. They are essential for good health and protection against illness and disease.

Spiritual blood is that of Jesus Christ. It is pure, spotless, without blemish, holy, just, righteous, and true. If you drink His blood, you will be saved. You will not perish. You are forgiven. You are debt-free. You are transformed with a renewed mind and have the power to exceed abundantly in the newness of life through the Blood.

There is power in the Blood of Jesus! He will keep you so no man or devil can overtake you. He will lead you in the right direction and protect you from seen and unseen dangers. His blood will bring about **sanctification, justification, and regeneration**.

Sanctification is a beginning process by grace, where a believer is separated from sin and becomes dedicated to GOD's righteousness, according to Romans 8:3-4. This is where the holiness and purification in your spiritual journey starts. This is where you become a new creature in Christ.

My water baptism was the most exciting day of my life. It was a day that I could never have imagined. The tears would not stop flowing from my eyes during the church service. Instantly, I knew it was the Power of God moving in my life. However, I did not know that there was a second baptism that needed to take place as well – the baptism of the Holy Ghost.

Water baptism is simply an outward expression or demonstration to the world of our acceptance of Christ. The Holy Ghost baptism washes and cleanses your heart, mind, body, and soul, which takes you into a deeper spiritual journey with GOD. This is where He reveals understanding, knowledge, and wisdom in Him.

This complete purification is what changes your demeanor, character, and morals. It also gives you the power to walk on top of your circumstances. It reveals the light of GOD that can not be hidden, for you are the salt of the world.

Justification is a process by which you are no longer

guilty of your wrongdoings. The debt of your sin was paid when Jesus died on the Cross. You are justified by having faith that Jesus' death is sufficient for your everlasting life.

Regeneration means that you have been made new. It is a spiritual change for a mortal person to become a new creature in oneness with Christ Jesus. It is the spiritual conversion from sinful acts. Through this process, you have a new walk, new talk, and a new lifestyle. The devil does not have you anymore. Remember, you can have fun and still live your life in the LORD!

Prayer

Father GOD,

In the name of your most sacred son, Jesus, who you sent to bear the Cross for me undeservedly, I confess with my mouth, an open heart, and humble shameful spirit that I have lived a destructive life full of wrongdoing. Today, I repent and ask for forgiveness. I surrender all of myself to you. I am leaning on your Word for my guidance. Thank you for everlasting life.

Amen

CHAPTER 10
LIVING A FRUITFUL LIFE IN SPIRIT

What comes to mind when you hear the phrase "be fruitful?" How would you express or describe it to someone? John 15:1 states, "I am the true vine, and my Father is the husbandman." Jesus is the True Vine in the vineyard. The following verse (John 15:2) says, "Every branch in me that beareth not fruit he taketh away: and every branch that beareth fruit, he purgeth it, that it may bring forth more fruit."

The vineyard represents the souls whom GOD has formed and fashioned in their mothers' wombs and breathed the "breath of life" into. We, in turn, must believe that Jesus is the True Living Vine. There must be a connection with Jesus by living, walking, and talking in holiness, peace, love, gentleness, kindness, patience, and joy in the Holy Ghost.

Have you ever felt the desire to be accepted, validated, or approved by family, friends, peers, significant others, or fellow believers? Have you ever spent years of your life trying to find the right connections? You tried the wisdom of the world, and there was no answer. You tried therapists, self-help books and abused drugs and alcohol. You even looked for love in the wrong places. Needless to say, nothing worked out on your behalf. You still found yourself on a dead-end path.

Jesus said, "If you abide in me, I'll abide in you." He is asking you to connect with Him. He is the answer to all of the problems in your life. He will fill that void, that dark lonely, empty place that no one else can fill. Let go and let GOD take complete control.

There is a safe haven in Jesus. If you dwell under the shadow of His wings, you will be connected in His love, peace, and righteousness. There will be trials and tribulations while you are connected with Christ, but He will keep you in His perfect peace in the midst of your storms. Jesus knows how to mend your broken heart. He will give you the power to stand on His Word, progress in His love, and keep a sound mind. Remember, God is always on your side.

<u>NOTES</u>

About the Author

Dr. Linda M. Washington has shared her recovery and divine intervention of substance abuse for 18 years, which compelled her to go deeper than the 12 Steps Principle. After living a life of substance dependence, she has been a living testimony for over 20 years of the healing and deliverance that can be accomplished through no other being than GOD Almighty himself.

Dr. Washington earned her Doctorate in Theology and Christian Counseling from Pneuma Theological Seminary, Oakland, CA. In addition, she pursued online studies as an Addiction Specialist at Breining Institute in Sacramento, CA. Linda is now qualified to discuss how addictions affect the brain, dual diagnosis, and coping skills.

Dr. Linda Washington volunteers in various recovery environments where she has facilitated group and counseling sessions within her community and among men and women in a homeless outreach and jail facility for the last 15 years.

When Linda is not operating in the capacity of an Addiction Specialist, she spends her time as an Evangelist teaching and preaching the gospel to a hurting community.

If you would like to book her services for public engagements or private interventions, she can be reached by email at LWASH502002@yahoo.com or DRLMW@outlook.com.

www.ingramcontent.com/pod-product-compliance
Lightning Source LLC
LaVergne TN
LVHW051812080426
835513LV00017B/1927